WHAT DOES IT DO?

WHAT DOES IT DO?
AMBULANCE
BY JOSH GREGORY

Published in the United States of America by Cherry Lake Publishing
Ann Arbor, Michigan
www.cherrylakepublishing.com

Content Adviser: Louis Teel, Professor of Heavy Equipment, Central Arizona College
Reading Adviser: Cecilia Minden-Cupp, PhD, Literacy Consultant

Photo Credits: Cover and page 1, ©Hodag Media/Shutterstock, Inc.; page 5,
©Ferguswang/Dreamstime.com; page 7, ©Robert Asento/Shutterstock, Inc.; page 9,
©iStockphoto.com/monkeybusinessimages; page 11, ©Lane Erickson/Dreamstime.com;
page 13, ©Pawel Nawrot/Shutterstock, Inc.; page 15, ©iStockphoto.com/nano; page 17,
©Pavel Losevsky/Dreamstime.com; page 19, ©iStockphoto.com/LSOphoto; page 21,
©Dreamshot/Dreamstime.com

LIBRARY OF CONGRESS CATALOGING-IN-PUBLICATION DATA
Gregory, Josh.
  What does it do? Ambulance/by Josh Gregory.
    p. cm.—(Community connections)
  Includes bibliographical references and index.
  ISBN-13: 978-1-60279-969-1 (lib. bdg.)
  ISBN-10: 1-60279-969-5 (lib. bdg.)
  1. Ambulances—Juvenile literature. 2. Ambulance service—Juvenile literature. I. Title.
II. Title: Ambulance. III. Series.
  TL235.8.G77 2010
  362.18'8—dc22   2010023579

Cherry Lake Publishing would like to acknowledge the
work of The Partnership for 21st Century Skills. Please
visit *www.21stcenturyskills.org* for more information.

Printed in the United States of America
Corporate Graphics Inc.
January 2011
CLSP08

AMBULANCE

CONTENTS

WHAT DOES IT DO?

CALL AN AMBULANCE!

You are having fun at the playground with your friend. "Ouch!" your friend yells. He has fallen off the jungle gym. He is hurt. You run and tell your mom what happened.

"Don't worry," she says. "I'll call an **ambulance**!"

Ambulances go anywhere someone is hurt.

Ambulances are special **vehicles**. They come when someone is hurt. Bright lights and **sirens** tell everyone that there is an **emergency**.

Car drivers move over to let the ambulance pass by. The ambulance must reach the hurt person as soon as possible.

Bad weather can't stop ambulances from reaching people who are sick or hurt.

THINK!

Drivers must pull over when they see an ambulance's lights. Drivers who do not pull over can get in trouble. Do you think this is an important rule? Why do you think so?

Paramedics and **emergency medical technicians (EMTs)** ride in the ambulance. EMTs know how to use an ambulance's tools. They treat some problems.

Paramedics have more training. They can treat many different kinds of problems.

Ambulance workers are always ready to help people in need of care.

EMTs and paramedics
need a lot of training.
Do you know any
EMTs or paramedics?
Ask them what they
needed to do before
starting their jobs.

9

The ambulance has arrived! First, the EMTs and paramedics find out what is wrong. They ask questions and look at the hurt person. Sometimes they start working on the person right away. Other times, they just need to take the person to a hospital.

Ambulances bring paramedics and EMTs to places where help is needed.

OFF TO THE HOSPITAL

Your friend has a broken arm. He needs to go to the hospital. The EMTs put him on a **stretcher**. A stretcher looks like a small bed. The EMTs lift it into the back of the ambulance. They strap it down to make sure it won't move around.

What might happen if a stretcher isn't strapped down in an ambulance?

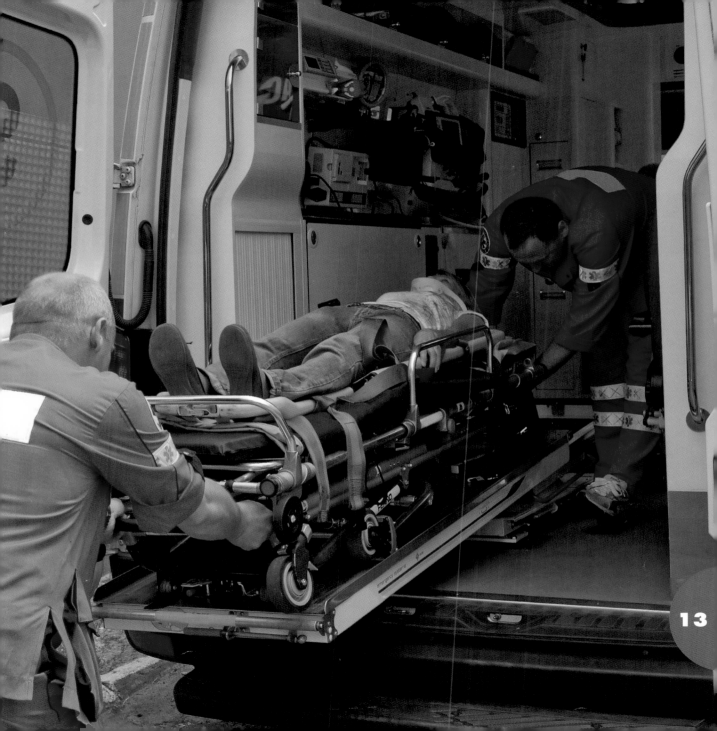

EMTs and paramedics work in teams. One person drives the ambulance. Other people ride in the back with the **patient**.

Sometimes people are hurt very badly. EMTs or paramedics might work on patients on the way to the hospital.

Working together can help save lives.

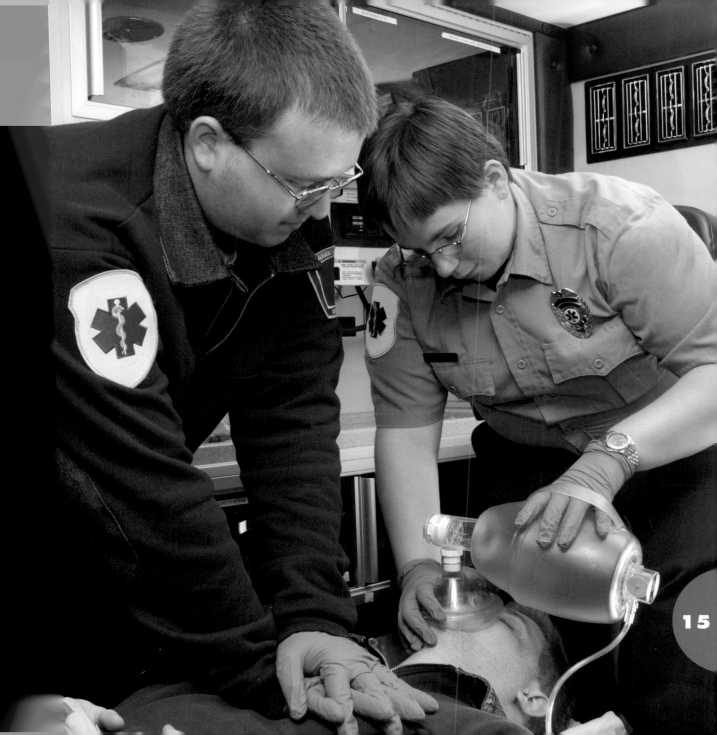

The back of an ambulance has many things that a hospital room does. That means there are a lot of tools packed into a small space.

There is **medicine**. There are also machines. These help the EMTs and paramedics take care of the patient.

Every bit of space counts inside an ambulance.

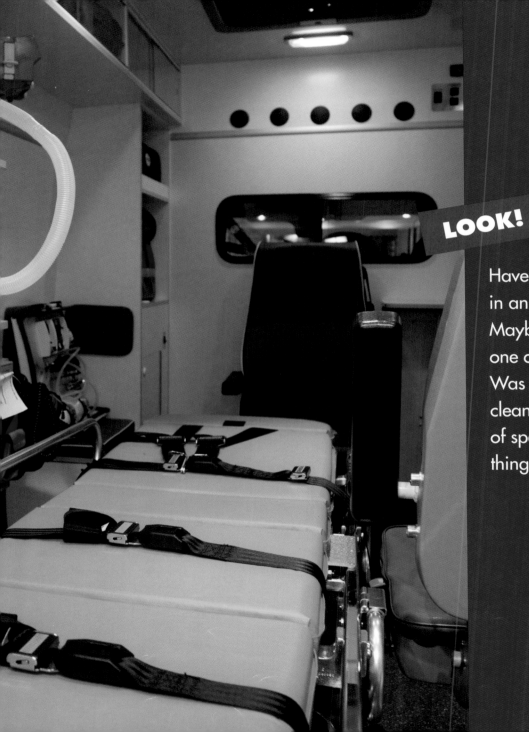

LOOK!

Have you ever ridden in an ambulance? Maybe you've seen one on a TV show. Was the ambulance clean? Was there a lot of space? What other things did you see?

17

The ambulance has to go very fast sometimes. It might need to race around cars. It might hit bumps.

Ambulances are built so things in the back don't shake around. The patient stays safe. All of the tools stay in their places.

Why is it important for ambulances to carry many different kinds of supplies?

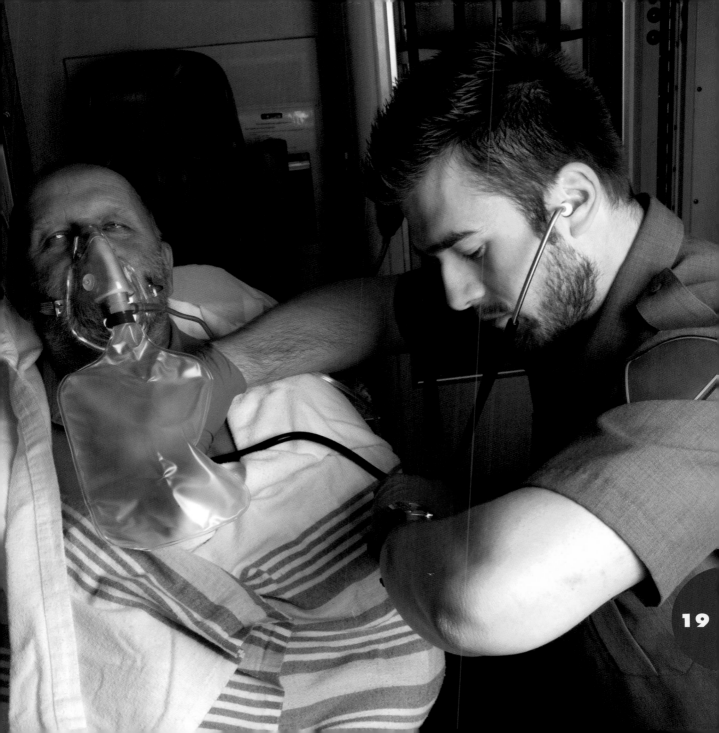

ALL BETTER!

The ambulance gets your friend to the hospital quickly. A doctor puts a cast on his arm. Soon he will be all better.

Now you know just how ambulances help people. Remember what they do next time you see one speeding down the street!

Ambulances from different places may look different. This ambulance is in Mexico.

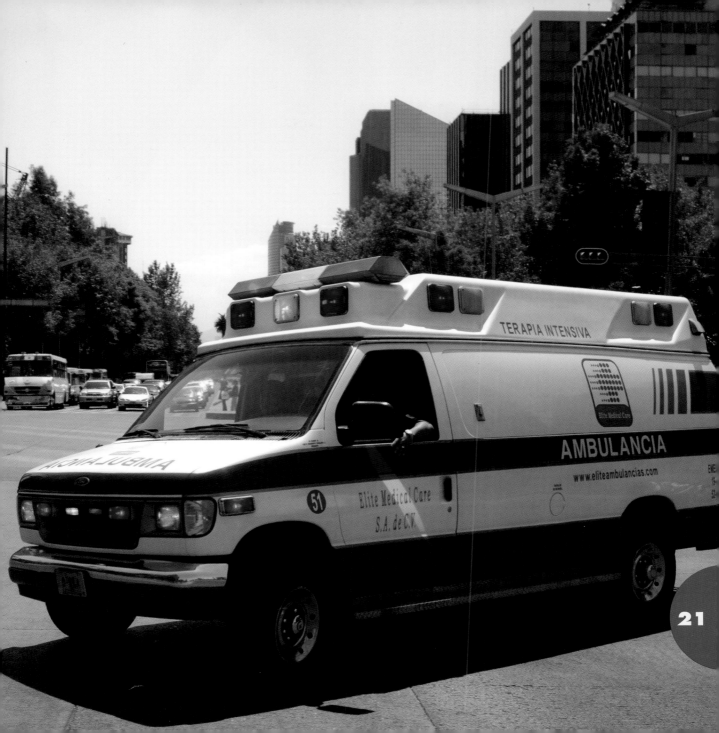

GLOSSARY

ambulance (AM-byuh-luhnss) a special vehicle for taking people to a hospital

emergency (i-MUR-juhn-see) a dangerous situation that must be taken care of very quickly

emergency medical technicians (EMTs) (i-MUR-juhn-see MED-ih-kuhl tek-NIH-shunz) people trained to help those who are sick or hurt

medicine (MED-uh-suhn) drugs used to help someone who is sick

paramedics (pa-ruh-MED-ikss) highly trained EMTs who can help treat patients' injuries

patient (PAY-shuhnt) a person getting medical help

sirens (SYE-ruhnz) objects that make loud noises to warn people of danger

stretcher (STRECH-er) a small bed that is used to move someone who is hurt

vehicles (VEE-uh-kuhlz) things that carry people or objects from one place to another, such as cars or trucks

FIND OUT MORE

BOOKS

Gordon, Sharon. *What's Inside an Ambulance?* New York: Marshall Cavendish Benchmark, 2007.

Manolis, Kay. *Ambulances*. Minneapolis: Bellwether Media, 2008.

Randolph, Joanne. *Ambulances*. New York: PowerKids Press, 2008.

WEB SITES

KidsHealth—What Happens in the Emergency Room?
kidshealth.org/kid/feel_better/places/er.html
Read more about what happens after an ambulance gets a patient to the hospital.

Science Channel Videos: How Do They Do It? Ambulances
science.discovery.com/videos/how-do-they-do-it-ambulances.html
Watch this interesting video to learn how ambulances are built and tested.

INDEX

ABOUT THE AUTHOR

Josh Gregory writes
and edits books
for kids. He lives in
Chicago, Illinois.